Young DREAMERS PRESS

VISIT US ONLINE AT:
WWW.YOUNGDREAMERSPRESS.COM

CHECK US OUT ON FACEBOOK!
WWW.FACEBOOK.COM/YOUNGDREAMERSPRESS

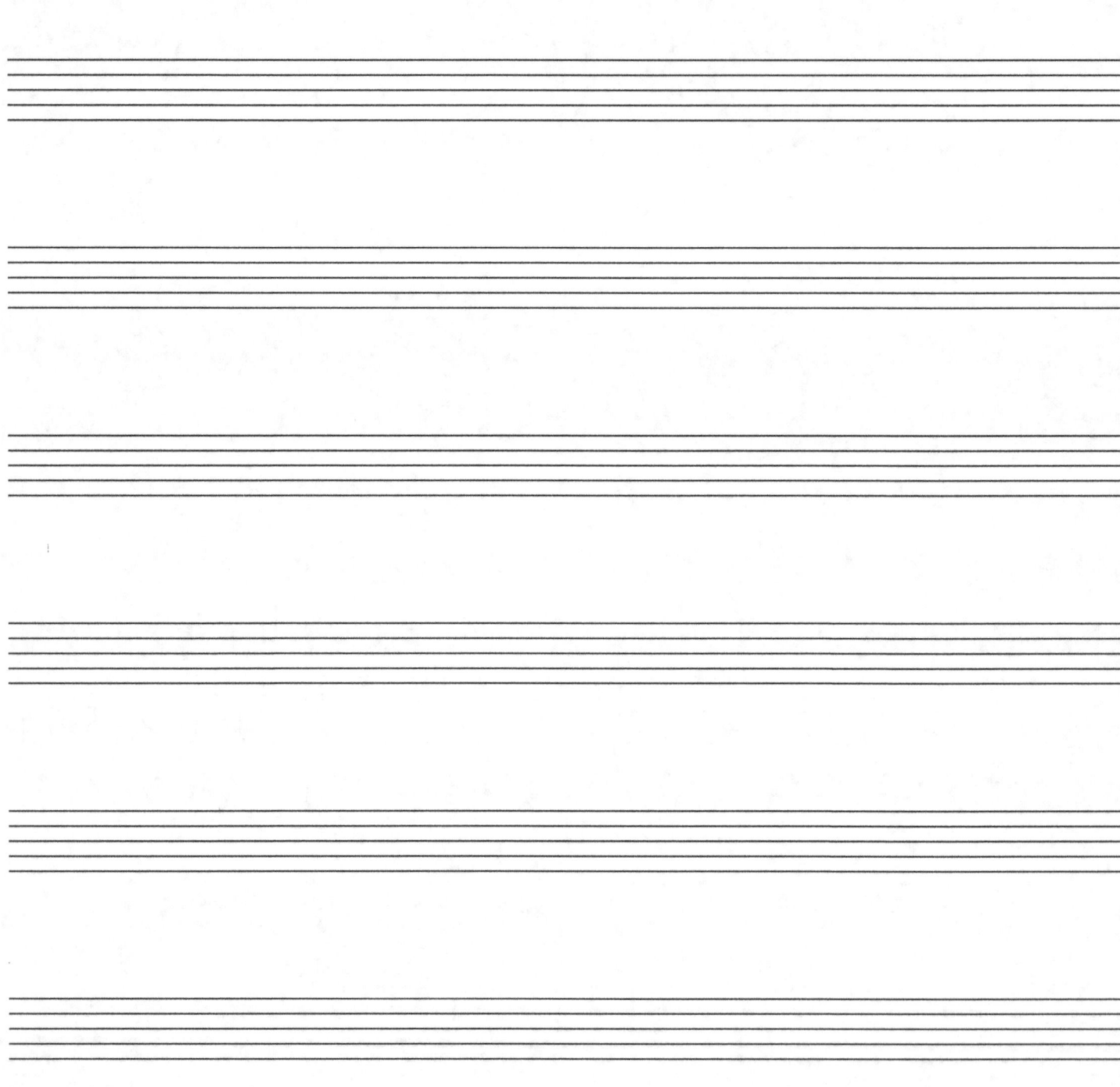

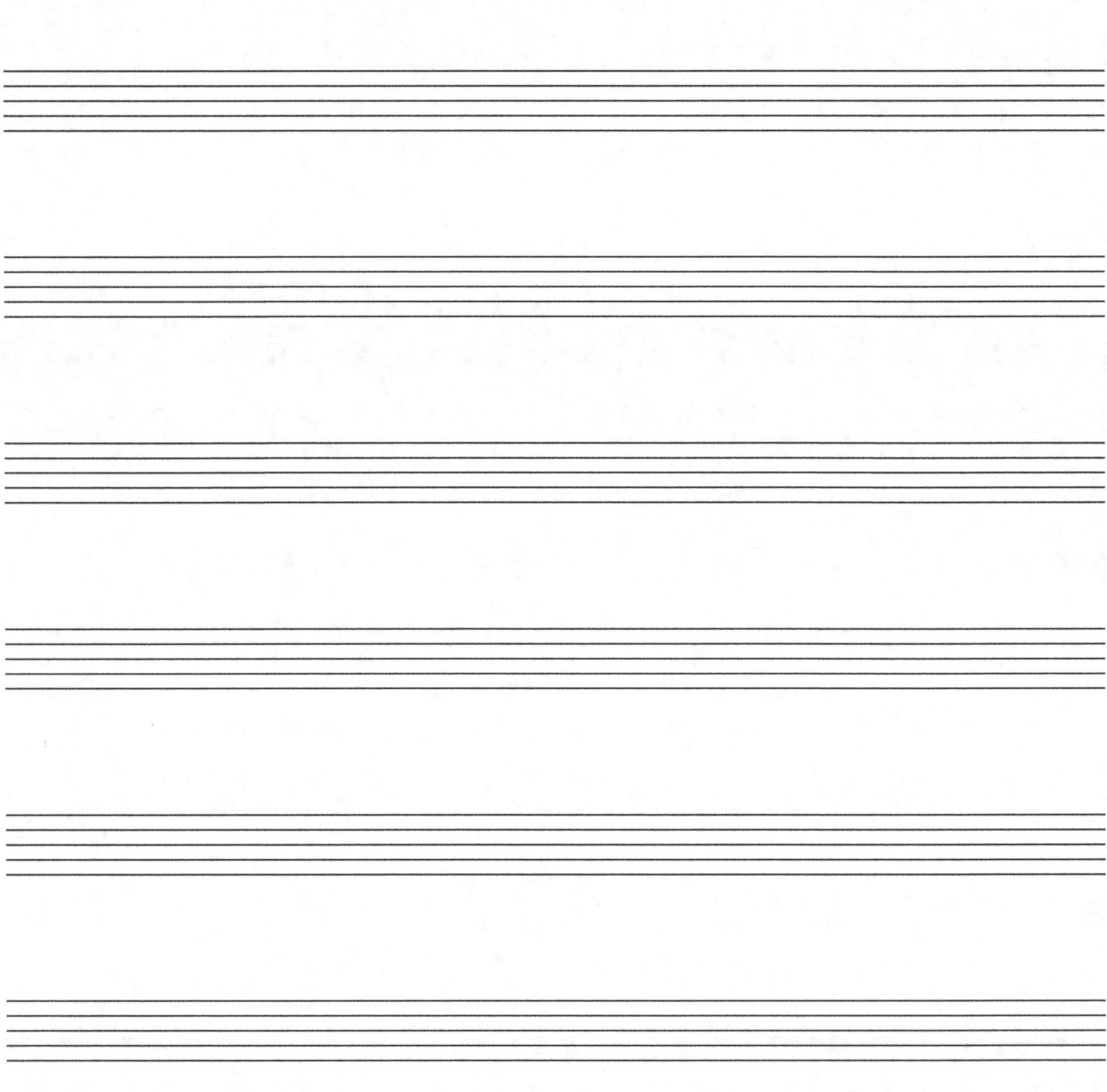

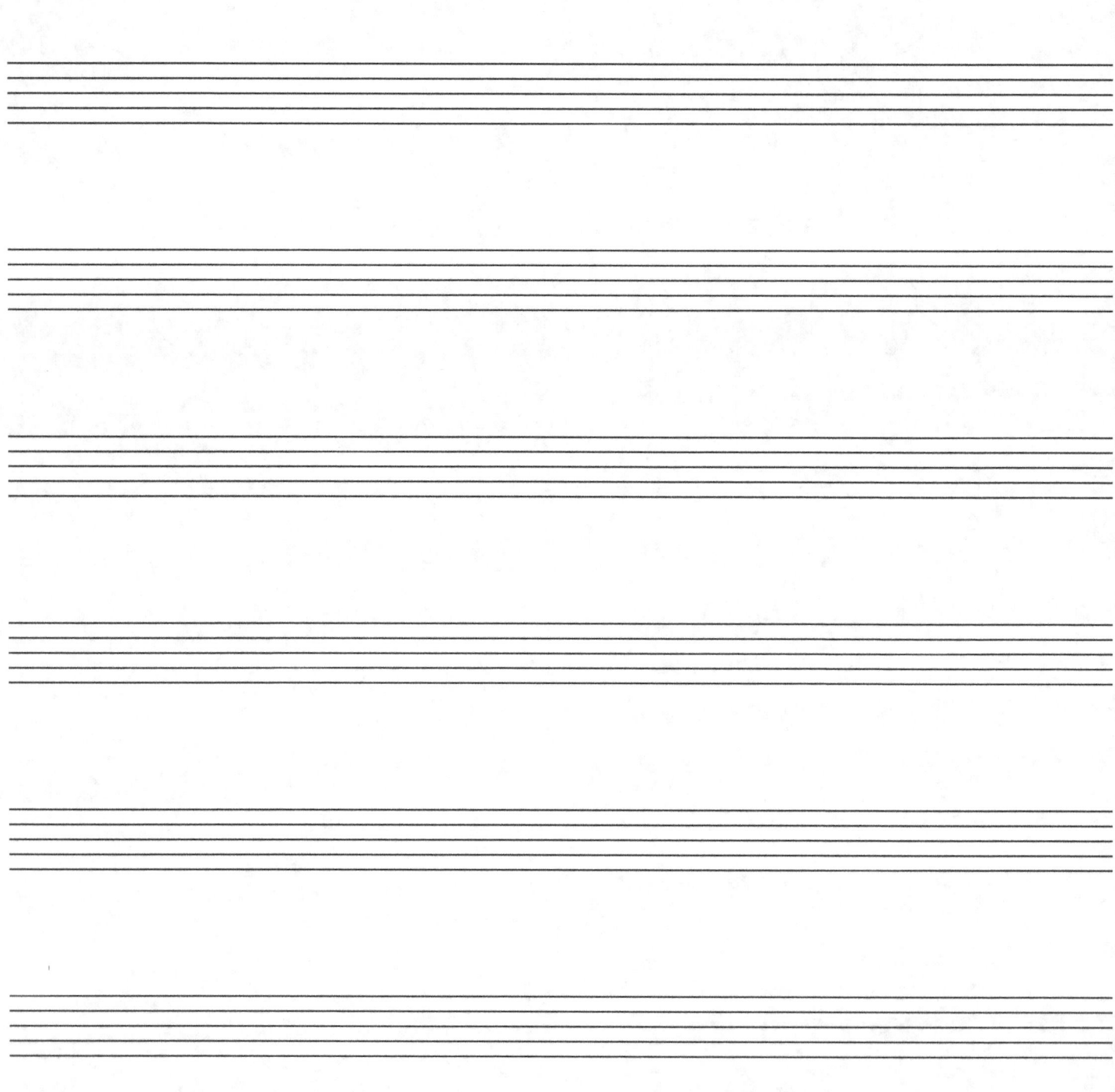

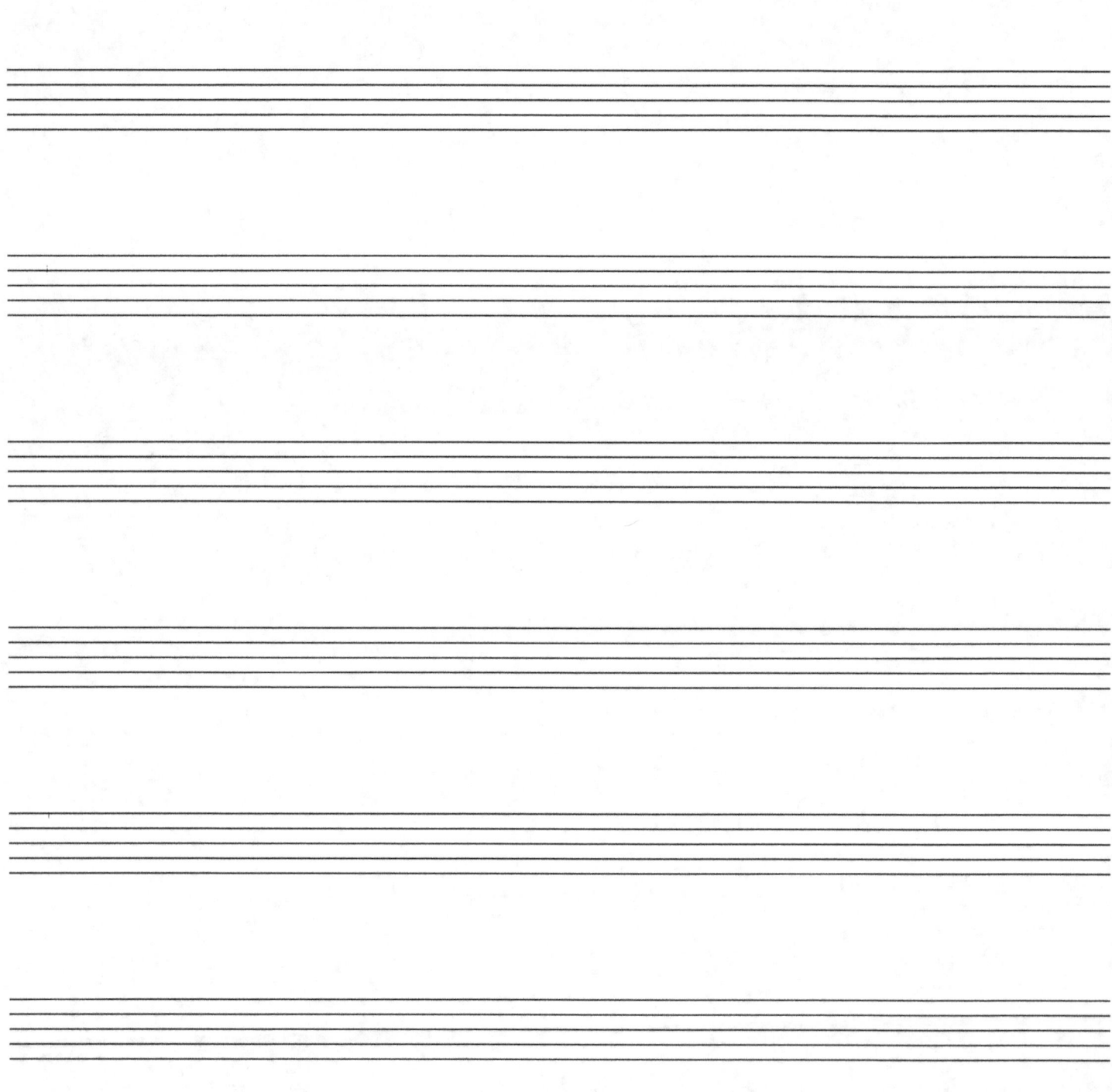

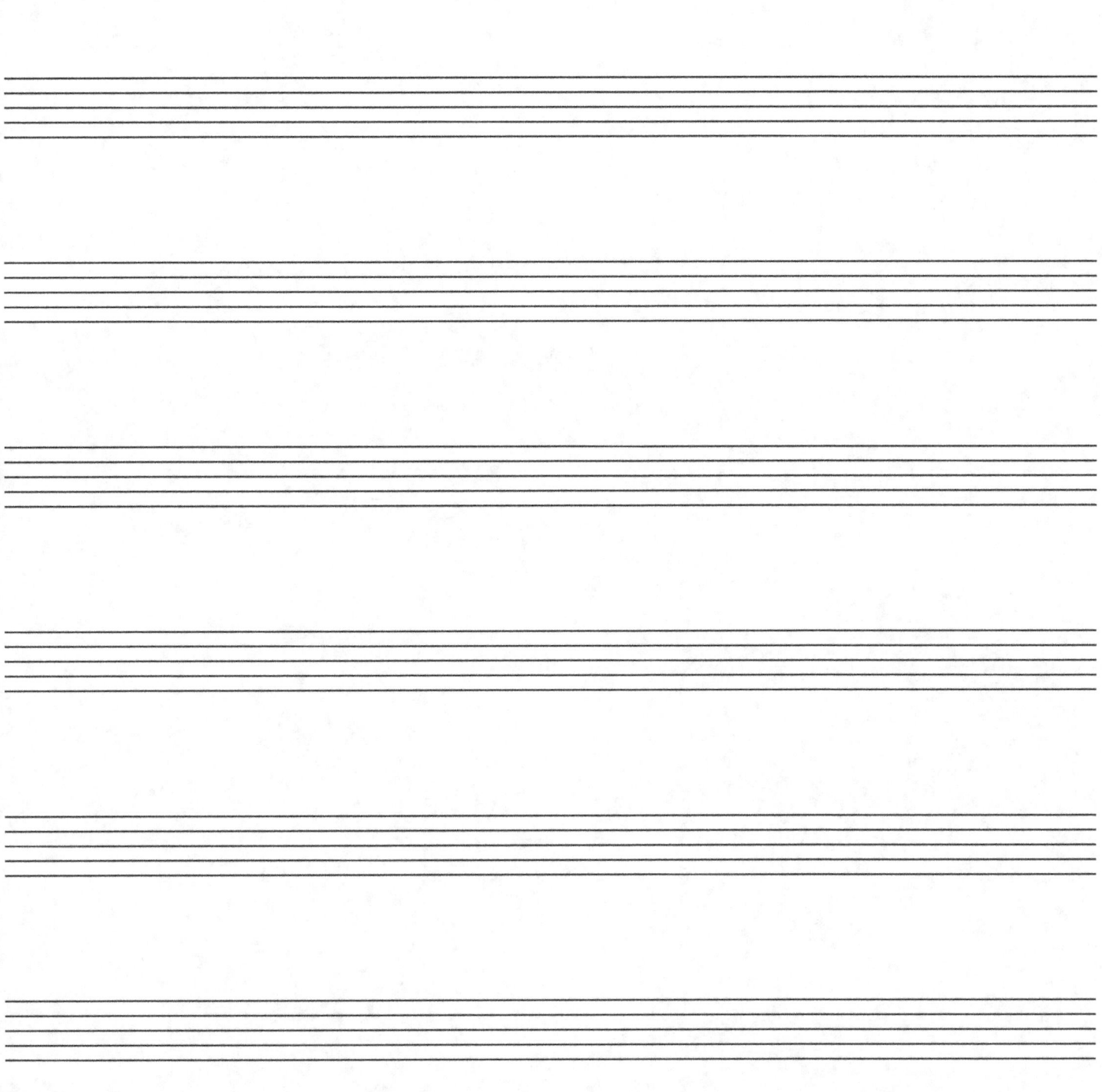

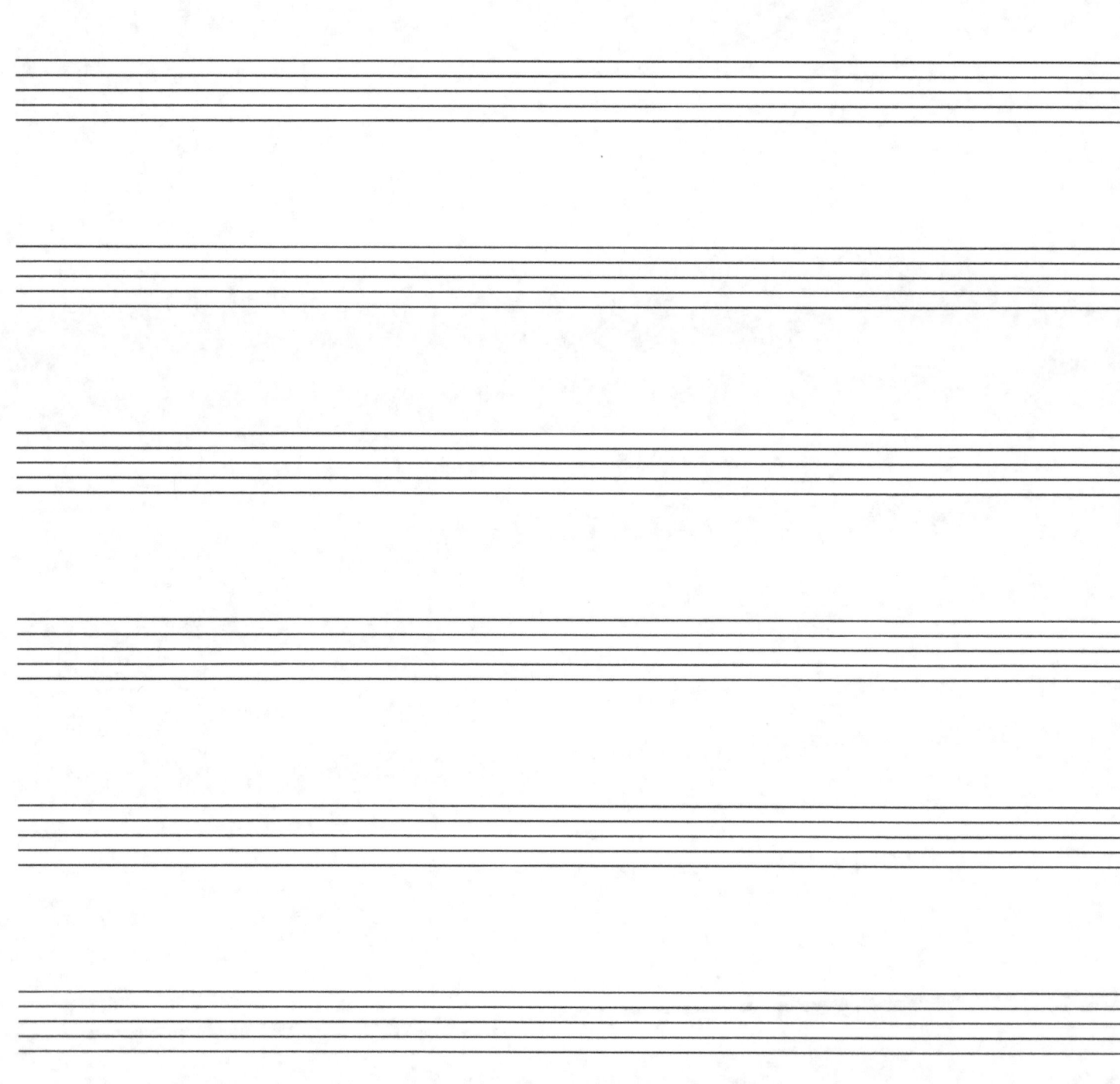

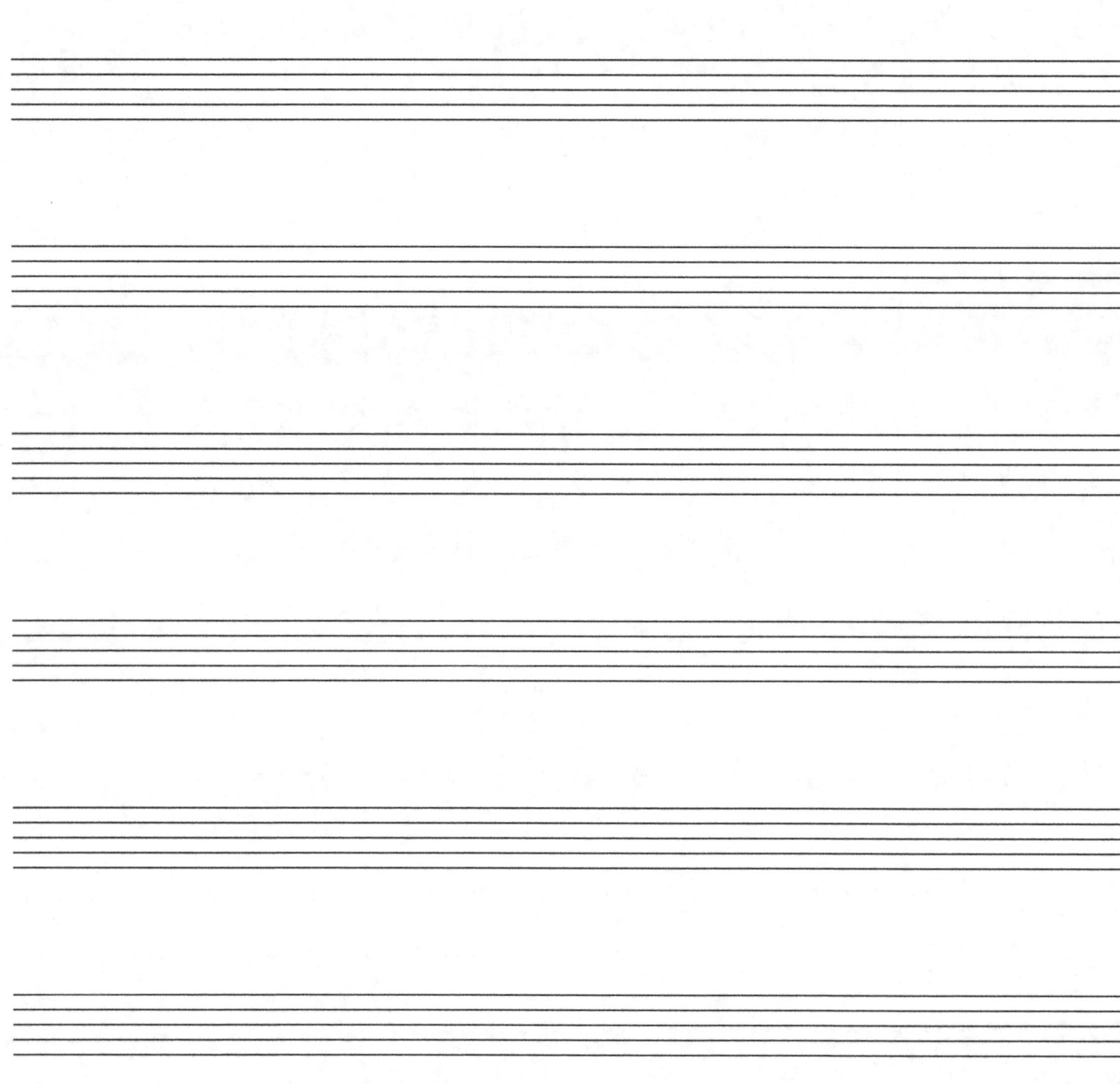

www.ingramcontent.com/pod-product-compliance
Lightning Source LLC
Chambersburg PA
CBHW081156070526
44583CB00021B/2872